I0810819

The INSIDE GUIDE

WOMEN IN U.S. HISTORY

Women in the Industrial Revolution

By Therese M. Shea

Cavendish Square

Published in 2025 by Cavendish Square Publishing, LLC
2544 Clinton Street Buffalo, NY 14224

First Edition

Website: cavendishsq.com

Library of Congress Cataloging-in-Publication Data

Names: Shea, Therese, author.
Title: Women in the Industrial Revolution / Therese M. Shea.
Description: New York : Cavendish Square Publishing, [2025] | Series: The inside guide: women in U.S. history | Audience term: Children
Identifiers: LCCN 2024026824 (print) | LCCN 2024026825 (ebook) | ISBN 9781502673183 (library binding) | ISBN 9781502673176 (paperback) | ISBN 9781502673190 (ebook)
Subjects: LCSH: Women employees–United States–History–Juvenile literature. | Industrial revolution–United States–History–Juvenile literature.
Classification: LCC HD6055.6.U6 S54 2025 (print) | LCC HD6055.6.U6 (ebook) | DDC 331.40973–dc23/eng/20240802
LC record available at https://lccn.loc.gov/2024026824
LC ebook record available at https://lccn.loc.gov/2024026825

Editor: Therese M. Shea
Copyeditor: Danielle Haynes
Designer: Deanna Lepovich

The photographs in this book are used by permission and through the courtesy of: Cover Shutterstock AI Generator/ Shutterstock.com; pp. 4, 12, 13 (main), 21, 23, 24 (left), 25 (inset), 26 courtesy of the Library of Congress; p. 6 EWY Media/ Shutterstock.com; p. 7 Javier Jaime/Shutterstock.com; p. 8 Hein Nouwens/Shutterstock.com; p. 9 Alethia Browning Tanner (page 70 crop)/Wikimedia Commons; p. 10 2 Young Women/Wikimedia Commons; p. 13 (inset) Lowell Offering 1/Wikimedia Commons; p. 15 ilbusca/iStock.com; pp. 16, 18, 29 (right) Everett Collection/Shutterstock.com; p. 19 FGA Constitution/Wikimedia Commons; p. 20 VOI Head (1847)/Wikimedia Commons; p. 22 American Waltham Watch Factory, W. A. Webster, photographer, c. 1880, from the Digital Commonwealth - 1 commonwealth mg74rs39m/Wikimedia Commons; p. 24 (right) Clara Lemlich 1910/ Wikimedia Commons; p. 25 (main) Image of Triangle Shirtwaist Factory fire on March 25 - 1911/Wikimedia Commons; p. 29 (left) NY shirtwaist workers strikers having lunch/Wikimedia Commons.

CPSIA compliance information: Batch #CWCSQ25: For further information contact Cavendish Square Publishing LLC at 1-877-980-4450.

Printed in the United States of America

CONTENTS

The Industrial Revolution began in Great Britain in the mid-1700s. Some historians mark its U.S. beginning in 1793, at a textile mill in Pawtucket, Rhode Island, shown here.

A TIME OF CHANGE

Chapter One

The word "revolution" has several meanings. One is a complete change in how people live. The Industrial Revolution in the United States was a time of tremendous transformation in homes and workplaces. Before this period, people mostly made or grew what they needed themselves. However, with the inventions of engine-powered machines (especially steam engines), people found faster ways of making goods and more of them. This led to huge changes in American **culture**, including in the place of women in society.

Machines Made It Happen

To understand the effects of the Industrial Revolution, it's helpful to understand life before it. In the United States, most people lived on farms or in rural communities. Cities existed but were much smaller than they are today. Most people didn't travel far from where they were born

Fast Fact

Many inventors contributed to the development of the steam engine. Scottish instrument maker James Watt made the steam engine much more effective in the late 1700s.

This cotton-spinning machine, called Arkwright's water frame, produced fine, strong thread.

Fast Fact

Steam engines made faster boats possible as well as locomotives. These vehicles and, later, gasoline-engine cars made it easier and faster to transport goods and people in the United States.

during their lives. They made their own clothing, tools, and other goods. They acquired things they couldn't make by trading with others. Life for all but the wealthy was filled with time-consuming tasks.

The engine-powered machinery of the Industrial Revolution ended this dependence on handmade goods. For example, making cloth was once

Many developments during the Industrial Revolution relied on the steam engine, shown here. As new machines were invented, steam engines became more powerful.

a lengthy task. Women had to spin wool or cotton to make yarn or thread. Then, they wove the thread together to make cloth. Inventors during the Industrial Revolution created machinery that could spin thread and yarn as well as weave and **mass-produce** cloth.

Besides speeding up processes and making mass-production possible, the Industrial Revolution started the factory system. A factory is a large building full of machinery where goods can be manufactured. Factories needed large workforces to operate the machinery.

As new machinery was introduced in agriculture, fewer laborers were able to produce more crops. Some people left farms and moved to cities looking for new opportunities in factories. This included

This early threshing machine separated seeds from plants. Before the machinery of the Industrial Revolution, farm work had to be done by hand. It was only possible with many laborers.

women, and many American women were introduced to work outside the home for the first time.

Fast Fact

The War of 1812, between the United States and Great Britain, sped up the U.S. Industrial Revolution. Americans wanted more and larger industries so they could import fewer goods from Great Britain and other nations.

Leaving Home

Before the Industrial Revolution, women mostly oversaw the home and children. They produced food, clothing, candles, and other household goods. They tended gardens too. Their role was critical but not paid. Some accepted outside work if they had to, such as mending and spinning fibers for neighbors.

After the start of the Industrial Revolution, though, things began to change. Many men left farm work because they couldn't support themselves or families. They sought factory work instead. Many young women soon followed out of economic necessity and because factories and mills sought them out. Some women wanted to help their families. Others wanted to be economically independent. No matter the reason, women's roles in the United States transformed.

CULTURAL EXPECTATIONS

Colonial America was a place in which women had few rights under the law. Married women had fewer rights than single or widowed women. Free Black women faced **discrimination** for being both women and Black, and enslaved Black women had no rights at all. American independence from Britain didn't change much for women's rights. Most women continued to be held back by a lack of education, controlling husbands and fathers, and a culture that didn't view them as equal. In fact, many women of this time didn't see themselves as equal to men.

In the early 1800s, Alethia Browning Tanner was an enslaved woman who sold vegetables out of her own garden. She eventually bought her own freedom (and others') and became a businesswoman. However, her experience was uncommon for Black women of that time.

Two young women who worked in the mills in Lowell, Massachusetts, are shown here in a photograph from around 1870. A mill is a building with machinery for manufacturing.

Chapter Two

THE WOMEN OF THE LOWELL MILLS

Boston, Massachusetts, merchant Francis Cabot Lowell had the idea of creating a community centered around textile production. The first mills of Lowell, Massachusetts, opened in 1823, on the Merrimack River. By 1843, Lowell was the nation's largest industrial center. Its many mills sought women workers.

Why Women?

Why did the employers of the Lowell mills want women especially? One reason is that they could pay women less money than men. They also believed they could control them more than men. They thought women would likely work only a few years. If they got married and had children, they'd leave. This was an advantage to the mill owners rather than a disadvantage because they thought women wouldn't be around long enough to grow unhappy with conditions or pay and organize into a labor group.

Fast Fact

Newspapers at the time called women who worked in mills "mill girls" or "factory operatives." An operative is another name for a worker who operates machinery.

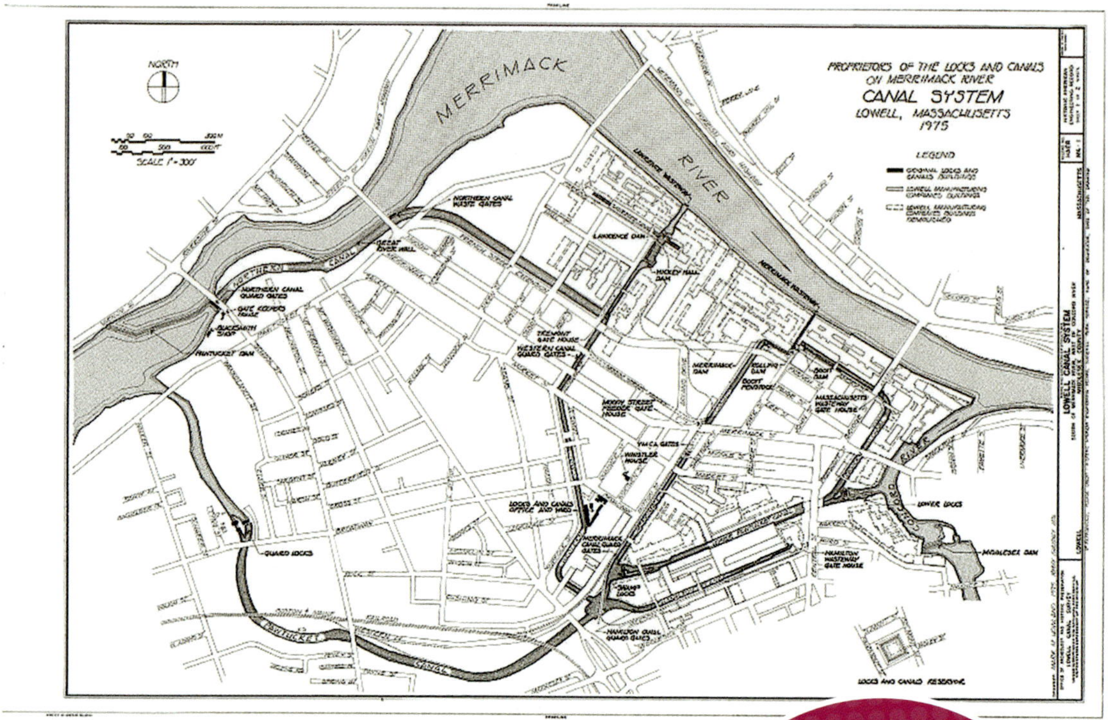

Business owners and investors had a series of canals (*above*) built to supply power needed to run the machinery of the Lowell mills.

Fast Fact

By 1843, almost 30,000 women worked at Lowell's 10 biggest textile businesses.

Why did women want to work at the mills? Many came from large farm families that were having a hard time making ends meet. They could help their family by working in the factory and sending money home. In addition, men were leaving farming communities for the same reason, so there were fewer men for women to marry in their home communities. Thousands of women left New England farms for opportunities in Lowell. Many had never been in a city before.

The *Lowell Offering* was a kind of monthly magazine for women workers. Workers contributed poetry, stories, and other kinds of writing.

THE

LOWELL OFFERING:

A REPOSITORY

OF

ORIGINAL ARTICLES ON VARIOUS SUBJECTS,

WRITTEN

BY FACTORY OPERATIVES.

"Full many a gem of purest ray serene,
The dark, unfathomed caves of ocean bear;
Full many a flower is born to blush unseen,
And waste its sweetness on the desert air."

No. 1. Price $6\frac{1}{4}$cts.

THIS NUMBER WHOLLY WRITTEN

BY FEMALES EMPLOYED IN THE MILLS.

CONTENTS:

LOWELL, MASS,
...A. WATSON, 15 CENTRAL STREET.
...d by Tower, in the angle of Central and Gorham sts.;
...rimack st. opposite Tremont Corporation.

The Lowell National Historical Park preserves some of the textile mills and living quarters of Lowell.

FINDING POWER IN NUMBERS

Women were earning money for themselves during the Industrial Revolution, sometimes for the first time in their lives, but they lacked power in society. They couldn't vote, for example. They weren't given managing positions in the factories and mills. When they married, any property or money that was theirs became their husband's, a legal standing called coverture. However, they began to fight for their rights. In some ways, the Lowell mills' control over women workers led to them organizing and fighting against poor conditions, long hours, and low wages. Workers lived together, so they were able to compare experiences and plan their protests.

Life of the Female Operative

Once hired by a Lowell mill, women lived in nearby mill-owned buildings. The mills controlled much of their lives. Bells told them when to arrive at work and when to leave. They had to be at home and in bed at a certain time. They shared rooms and even beds with other workers. They had to attend church services too. Behavior considered improper could lead to a worker's firing.

Life at work was hard. Women worked up to 14 hours a day, with a half day on Saturday and Sunday off. As more textile companies were built around the nation, the price of cloth fell. To make more money, textile companies made workers handle more machines at greater speeds. Accidents were common. Loud machines caused some workers to lose their hearing. In addition, **unventilated** workplaces contributed to the spread of illnesses and diseases.

In this photograph of a later cotton mill, you can see how uncovered and moving machinery gears could cause injuries. This was a part of everyday life in a mill or factory during the Industrial Revolution.

Fast Fact

Brown lung disease was an illness that affected Lowell mill workers. It was caused by breathing in cotton dust and could be fatal.

Lowell mill owners lowered wages when they wanted to. In 1834, they did so by 12.5 percent. When women tried to organize a strike, their leader, Julia Wilson, was fired. Wilson still managed to get 800 workers from Lowell mills to walk out of their jobs to protest the pay cut. However, the strike soon fell apart, and the women, needing the money, returned to work. The mill owners called the strikers "unwomanly." Seventy were fired and **blacklisted**.

From 1850 to 1900, between 16 and 23 percent of women had jobs in manufacturing. Many other women worked in mines and as domestic servants.

LABOR LEADERS

Chapter Three

During the Industrial Revolution, working-class women in other U.S. cities experienced much the same treatment as those in Lowell: low wages, long workdays, dangerous conditions, and no bargaining power. In some places in the South, mills constructed villages for workers' families. These enabled laborers to marry and have children but still live close to work. Wages were still low, though, and life wasn't easy.

Women whose husbands did factory work often had to work outside of the home because the average factory worker didn't earn enough for the survival of his family. Women often had their domestic work to do on top of their work at the factory or mill. Their children sometimes joined the workforce, though they were paid even less and worked as long a day as their parents.

Fast Fact

In 1890, just 45 percent of American workers earned a yearly income above the poverty level. Most families needed as many family members working as possible.

Obstacles to Organizing

Business owners who employed women made it hard for them to organize or protest. They threatened to fire them. They also threatened to tell other companies about their activities so they wouldn't be hired anywhere else.

A changing and unstable workforce was also a challenge. Since many women left the workforce to marry, it was hard to create a permanent organization and work toward long-term goals. Also, as the 19th century progressed, more immigrants moved into the country, looking for any employment they could find. They could replace striking workers and

Fast Fact

A mill worker named Sarah Bagley became president of the Lowell Female Labor Reform Association. An early supporter of the Lowell mill system, she later said, "I am sick at heart when I look into the social world and see woman so willingly made a dupe [fool] to the beastly selfishness of man."

Many immigrants who moved to the United States in the 1800s and early 1900s didn't know English. Factory and business owners took advantage of this as well as immigrants' poverty.

accepted the lowest-paying jobs because they had to. Despite these challenges, certain courageous women knew that, together, women workers had the power to force change.

First U.S. Women's Labor Union

Around 1845, the Lowell Female Labor Reform Association formed, with hundreds of women as members. This group worked with men's labor organizations to create change. Among its first goals was a 10-hour workday. About 2,000 workers **petitioned** the Massachusetts state legislature in 1845 to create a law making it illegal for businesses to force their workers to work longer than 10 hours in a day. This petition joined the petitions of many other **labor unions**.

While change was slow, the Lowell Female Labor Reform Association added chapters, or branches, in nearby towns and presented

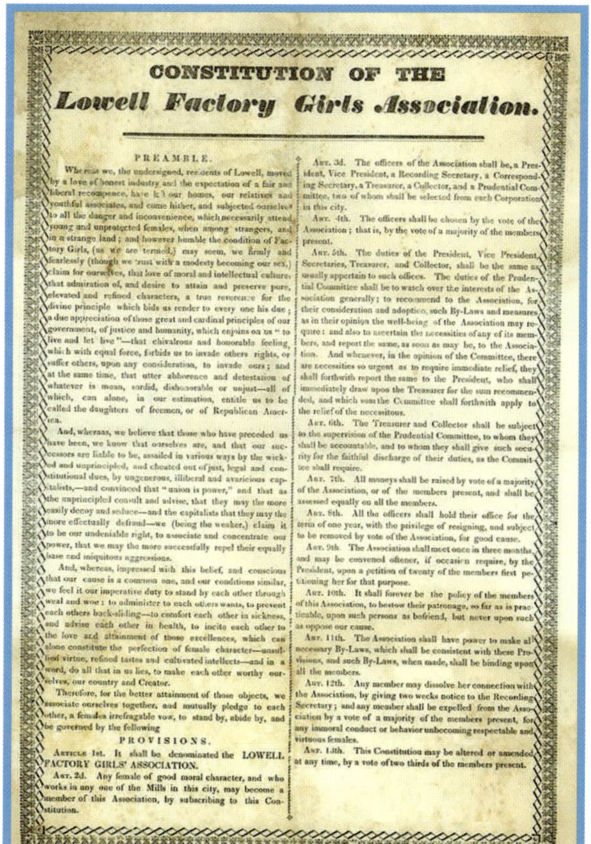

CONSTITUTION OF THE

Lowell Factory Girls Association.

PREAMBLE.

Whereas we, the undersigned, residents of Lowell, moved by a love of honest industry and the expectation of a fair and liberal recompence, have left our homes, our relatives and youthful associates, and come hither, and subjected ourselves to all the danger and inconvenience, which necessarily attend young and unprotected females, when among strangers, and in a strange land; and however humble the condition of Factory Girls, (as we are termed,) may seem, we firmly and fearlessly (though we trust with a modesty becoming our sex,) claim for ourselves, that love of moral and intellectual culture, that admiration of, and desire to attain and preserve pure, elevated and refined characters, a true reverence for the divine principle which bids us render to every one his due; a due appreciation of those great and cardinal principles of our government, of justice and humanity, which enjoins on us "to live and let live"—that chivalrous and honorable feeling, which with equal force, forbids us to invade others rights, or suffer others, upon any consideration, to invade ours; and at the same time, that utter abhorence and detestation of whatever is mean, sordid, dishonorable or unjust—all of which, can alone, in our estimation, entitle us to be called the daughters of freemen, or of Republican America.

And, whereas, we believe that those who have preceded us have been, we know that ourselves are, and that our successors are liable to be, assailed in various ways by the wicked and unprincipled, and cheated out of just, legal and constitutional dues, by ungenerous, illiberal and avaricious capitalists,—and convinced that "union is power," and that as the unprincipled consult and advise, that they may the more easily decoy and seduce—and the capitalists that they may the more effectually defraud—we (being the weaker,) claim it to be our undeniable right, to associate and concentrate our power, that we may the more successfully repel their equally base and iniquitous aggressions.

And, whereas, impressed with this belief, and conscious that our cause is a common one, and our conditions similar, we feel it our imperative duty to stand by each other through weal and woe: to administer to each others wants, to prevent each others back-sliding—to comfort each other in sickness, and advise each other in health, to incite each other to the love and attainment of those excellences, which can alone constitute the perfection of female character—unsullied virtue, refined tastes and cultivated intellects—and in a word, do all that in us lies, to make each other worthy ourselves, our country and Creator.

Therefore, for the better attainment of those objects, we associate ourselves together, and mutually pledge to each other, a females irrefragable vow, to stand by, abide by, and be governed by the following

PROVISIONS.

ARTICLE 1st. It shall be denominated the LOWELL FACTORY GIRLS' ASSOCIATION.

ART. 2d. Any female of good moral character, and who works in any one of the Mills in this city, may become a member of this Association, by subscribing to this Constitution.

ART. 3d. The officers of the Association shall be, a President, Vice President, a Recording Secretary, a Corresponding Secretary, a Treasurer, a Collector, and a Prudential Committee, two of whom shall be selected from each Corporation in this city.

ART. 4th. The officers shall be chosen by the vote of the Association; that is, by the vote of a majority of the members present.

ART. 5th. The duties of the President, Vice President, Secretaries, Treasurer, and Collector, shall be the same as usually appertain to such offices. The duties of the Prudential Committee shall be to watch over the interests of the Association generally; to recommend to the Association, for their consideration and adoption, such By-Laws and measures as in their opinion the well-being of the Association may require: and also to ascertain the necessities of any of its members, and report the same, as soon as may be, to the Association. And whenever, in the opinion of the Committee, there are necessities so urgent as to require immediate relief, they shall forthwith report the same to the President, who shall immediately draw upon the Treasurer for the sum recommended, and which sum the Committee shall forthwith apply to the relief of the necessitous.

ART. 6th. The Treasurer and Collector shall be subject to the supervision of the Prudential Committee, to whom they shall be accountable, and to whom they shall give such security for the faithful discharge of their duties, as the Committee shall require.

ART. 7th. All moneys shall be raised by vote of a majority of the Association, or of the members present, and shall be assessed equally on all the members.

ART. 8th. All the officers shall hold their office for the term of one year, with the privilege of resigning, and subject to be removed by vote of the Association, for good cause.

ART. 9th. The Association shall meet once in three months, and may be convened oftener, if occasion require, by the President, upon a petition of twenty of the members first petitioning her for that purpose.

ART. 10th. It shall forever be the policy of the members of this Association, to bestow their patronage, so far as is practicable, upon such persons as befriend, but never upon such as oppose our cause.

ART. 11th. The Association shall have power to make all necessary By-Laws, which shall be consistent with these Provisions, and such By-Laws, when made, shall be binding upon all the members.

ART. 12th. Any member may dissolve her connection with the Association, by giving two weeks notice to the Recording Secretary; and any member shall be expelled from the Association by a vote of a majority of the members present, for any immoral conduct or behavior unbecoming respectable and virtuous females.

ART. 13th. This Constitution may be altered or amended at any time, by a vote of two thirds of the members present.

The Lowell Female Labor Reform Association (later, the Lowell Female Industrial Reform and Mutual Aid Society) had a constitution. In it, its members stated their purpose was to secure "reasonable hours for manual [physical] labor" so that time was left for education and other pursuits.

The *Voice of Industry* newspaper featured articles about workplace conditions and policies as well as issues such as slavery and war. It was published from 1845 to 1848.

Fast Fact

Labor strikes sometimes turned violent. In 1887, a three-week-long strike against working conditions on a Louisiana sugarcane farm ended when white employers and militia killed about 60 Black workers, including women and children. This is called the Thibodaux Massacre.

issues to state legislatures. It also published a newspaper called the *Voice of Industry* and printed other materials to spread the word about mistreatment in mills and factories.

Massachusetts eventually passed the first enforceable 10-hour workday law in 1874, though it was only for women and child workers. By this time, the Second Industrial Revolution had started. Beginning around 1870, new advancements were made in manufacturing, **technology** and industrial production. Women remained a substantial part of the workforce.

EXCLUDED

Many industries of the Industrial Revolution largely excluded, or left out, Black and other non-European women. These women found jobs in services, such as cooking, cleaning, and laundry. They, too, fought for fair treatment in their jobs. In 1881, Black laundry workers in Atlanta, Georgia, led by Carrie Steele Logan, went on strike for higher wages, one of the first recorded strikes by American Black women. They won their demands. In 1917, Nannie Helen Burroughs founded the National Association of Wage Earners to help Black domestic workers fight for fair wages and working conditions. It grew to include 23 chapters and as many as 10,000 members.

Nannie Burroughs also founded a school for Black children in Washington, D.C., to help prepare them for careers other than in domestic service.

The Industrial Revolution created a large working class in the United States, which, in turn, meant a rise in labor unions to represent working-class people.

INTO THE 20TH CENTURY

Chapter Four

By the early 1900s, women were firmly established in the U.S. workforce. They were needed by various industries and services and yet were still treated unequally to male workers. This denial of civil rights helped push the women's rights movement that eventually led to women gaining the right to vote. Women labor leaders became some of the most famous faces of the U.S. labor movement.

"The Most Dangerous Woman"

Mary Harris "Mother" Jones was a dressmaker who came to the United States from Ireland as a young child. After she lost her dress shop in a fire in 1871, she became involved in a labor organization called the Knights of Labor. She soon became one

A lawyer once called Mother Jones "the most dangerous woman in America" because of the influence she had over labor unions and striking workers.

Fast Fact

The people for whom Mary Harris Jones fought loved her. They nicknamed her "Mother" out of respect.

of the most well-known labor **activists** in the nation, taking part in hundreds of strikes.

Mother Jones traveled the country and was a powerful speaker for unions. She also organized a march of about 100 child workers to President Theodore Roosevelt's home in 1903.

Garment Workers

In 1909, the largest women's labor strike in U.S history yet took place. More than 20,000 workers, mostly Jewish women, held an 11-week strike for New York's shirtwaist industry. (A shirtwaist was a kind of woman's blouse.) This was called the Uprising of the 20,000. The strike ended with some clear gains, such as a 52-hour

Famous garment activists included Rose Schneiderman (*left*) and Clara Lemlich (*right*). Both also fought for women's right to vote, which would improve their ability to fight for fair treatment in the workplace.

Fast Fact

By the end of the Uprising of the 20,000 strike, the membership of the International Ladies Garment Workers Union swelled from 100 to 10,000.

workweek and four paid holidays a year. New unions were established to support female garment workers.

A tragedy at a New York City factory in 1911 brought labor conditions into the national spotlight. The Triangle Shirtwaist factory fire lasted just 18 minutes, but 146 workers died, mostly young women.

The garment workers were on the 8th, 9th, and 10th floors of the building. A door to the stairway was locked to prevent workers from taking breaks, which kept workers from being able to escape to safety.

Frances Perkins (*right*) witnessed the Triangle Shirtwaist fire (*above*). She committed herself to helping the working class and later was named President Franklin D. Roosevelt's secretary of labor, the first woman in a presidential cabinet.

CHILDREN AT RISK

Some factory owners employed children for much the same reasons as they employed women. They could pay children less. Children were easily controlled and less likely to organize against management. Children's small fingers could operate certain kinds of machinery more easily too. However, children were also more likely to get injured in the workplace. Still, many parents felt forced to pull their children out of school, which wasn't required at the time, to have them work in factories and contribute to the family income. Children as young as 4 years old worked long days in dangerous places.

Fast Fact

In 1900, about 18 percent of U.S. workers were under the age of 16. It wasn't until 1938 that a federal law made it illegal for businesses to hire children younger than 16.

This 1910 photograph shows 12-year-old Addie Card working in a cotton mill in Vermont.

Some Triangle Shirtwaist factory workers jumped from the windows. After the fire, the public demanded change, and many new labor laws followed.

A Permanent Part of the Workforce

By the early 1900s, the United States had become the world's leading economy. The Second Industrial Revolution came to an end around the start of World War I, which erupted in 1914. Advances in technology, transportation, and communication continued, however.

Millions of women had entered the U.S. labor force by this time. Without their work, the nation couldn't have achieved such a level of economic success. Yet, the workplace would continue to challenge women with discrimination, dangers, and abuses. It would take many years—and many women labor leaders—to overcome these obstacles. This work continues today.

A TIMELINE OF WOMEN IN THE U.S. INDUSTRIAL REVOLUTION

1823
The Lowell mills and factories begin to recruit women workers.

1834
Lowell mill owners cut women's wages, sparking the first women's strike there.

1844
Mill worker Sarah Bagley becomes president of the newly founded Lowell Female Labor Reform Association.

1874
Massachusetts passes the first enforceable 10-hour workday law for women and child workers.

1881
Black laundry workers in Atlanta, Georgia, begin one of the first recorded strikes by Black American women.

1903
Mother Jones organizes a protest march of child workers to President Theodore Roosevelt's home.

1909
More than 20,000 women garment workers hold an 11-week strike in New York's shirtwaist district, winning some of their demands.

1911
A fire at the Triangle Shirtwaist factory kills 146 workers, mostly young women, which inspires new labor laws.

1917
Nannie Helen Burroughs founds the National Association of Wage Earners.

THINK ABOUT IT!

1. Why do you think women accepted being paid less than men?
2. What do you think Lowell mill owners meant when they called strikers "unwomanly"?
3. Why might historians link women joining the workforce and women fighting for the right to vote?
4. Why do you think many labor unions for men were unwilling to accept women at first?

GLOSSARY

activist: A person who uses or supports strong actions to help make changes in politics or society.

blacklist: To place someone on a list of persons who are disapproved of or are to be punished or boycotted.

cabinet: A group of senior officials appointed by the president as special advisers.

culture: The beliefs and ways of life of a group of people.

discrimination: Unfairly treating people unequally because of their gender, race, or beliefs.

domestic: Of the home, or dealing with skills, chores, or pursuits that have to do with the house.

labor union: A group of workers who join together to argue for better benefits.

mass-produce: To produce in large numbers, usually by machinery.

militia: A group of citizens who organize like soldiers in order to fight.

petition: Making a written request, signed by many people, asking a government to take an action. Also, the written request.

technology: The use science, engineering, and other industries to invent useful tools and processes or to solve problems. Also, the tools and processes invented.

textile: Cloth or fabric that is made by weaving thread together.

unventilated: Not allowing air to move in and through a space.

FIND OUT MORE

Books

Faust, Daniel R. *The Industrial Revolution*. Minneapolis, MN: Bearport Publishing, 2024.

Price-Wright, Heather. *Industrializing the United States*. Huntington Beach, CA: Teacher Created Materials, 2020.

Websites

Ducksters: Industrial Revolution: How It Began in the United States
www.ducksters.com/history/us_1800s/united_states_industrial_revolution.php
Check out this review of major events of the Industrial Revolution.

National Park Service: 200 Years of Labor History
www.nps.gov/blrv/learn/historyculture/200-labor-events.htm
Read about the strikes and other events that have shaped labor in the United States.

The Role of Women in the Industrial Revolution
www.uml.edu/tsongas/barilla-taylor/women-industrial-revolution.aspx
Check out more about this subject, especially the women of the Lowell mills.

INDEX